The Great Migration

American history, Volume 20

Michael Johnson

Published by Harmony House Publishing, 2024.

While every precaution has been taken in the preparation of this book, the publisher assumes no responsibility for errors or omissions, or for damages resulting from the use of the information contained herein.

THE GREAT MIGRATION

First edition. April 5, 2024.

Copyright © 2024 Michael Johnson.

ISBN: 979-8224376100

Written by Michael Johnson.

Table of Contents

To all those who embarked on the courageous journey from the South to the North, seeking freedom, opportunity, and a better life. Your resilience, sacrifice, and determination paved the way for generations to come. This book is dedicated to your enduring legacy and the profound impact of the Great Migration on American history and culture.

Chapter 1: Introduction

The Great Migration of African Americans from the South to the North was not a spontaneous event but rather a response to a complex set of socio-political and economic conditions that emerged in the aftermath of the Civil War. In this chapter, we will delve into the historical context of the South following the end of slavery, examining the push and pull factors that ultimately drove millions of African Americans to seek new opportunities and freedoms in the North.

Section 1: The Post-Civil War South

Following the Civil War and the abolition of slavery with the Emancipation Proclamation in 1863 and the ratification of the 13th Amendment in 1865, the Southern United States underwent a period of profound transformation. The end of slavery brought about significant changes in the social, economic, and political landscape of the region.

1.1 Reconstruction and its Challenges

The period of Reconstruction, which lasted from 1865 to 1877, aimed to rebuild the Southern states and integrate newly freed African Americans into society as equal citizens. However, Reconstruction faced numerous challenges, including resistance from white Southerners who sought to maintain their dominance and control over African Americans.

1.2 Rise of Black Codes and Jim Crow Laws

Despite the abolition of slavery, African Americans in the South continued to face systemic oppression and discrimination. In response to the newly gained freedom of African Americans, Southern states enacted a series of laws known as Black Codes, which aimed to restrict the rights and mobility of African Americans, effectively perpetuating a system of racial hierarchy and subjugation. These laws laid the groundwork for the later establishment of Jim Crow laws, which enforced racial segregation and further marginalized African Americans in all aspects of life.

1.3 Economic Exploitation and Sharecropping

Economic opportunities for African Americans in the South were severely limited in the post-Civil War era. Many former slaves found themselves trapped in a cycle of poverty and debt, as they were forced to rely on sharecropping and tenant farming to make a living. Under this system, African American farmers worked land owned by white landowners in exchange for a share of the crops produced, but often found themselves indebted to landlords due to exploitative contracts and unfair practices.

Section 2: Push and Pull Factors of the Great Migration

The Great Migration was not a singular event but rather a series of waves of African American migration from the South to the North that occurred over several decades, beginning in the late 19th century and continuing into the early 20th century. This mass movement of people was driven by a combination of push factors that compelled African Americans to leave the South and pull factors that attracted them to the North.

2.1 Push Factors

Push factors were the conditions and circumstances in the South that made life untenable for African Americans and compelled them to seek opportunities elsewhere. These included:

- Racial Violence and Segregation: African Americans in the South faced widespread racial violence and discrimination, including lynchings, mob attacks, and legal segregation. The threat of violence and the denial of basic civil rights pushed many African Americans to seek refuge in the North, where they hoped to find greater safety and freedom.

- Economic Disadvantages: The economic opportunities available to African Americans in the South were limited by the legacy of slavery and the oppressive sharecropping system. Many African Americans struggled to make ends meet and saw little hope for economic advancement in the South.

- Political Disenfranchisement: African Americans in the South were systematically disenfranchised through voter suppression tactics such as poll taxes, literacy tests, and grandfather clauses. The lack of political representation left African Americans powerless to effect change and address the injustices they faced.

2.2 Pull Factors

Pull factors were the opportunities and advantages offered by the North that attracted African Americans seeking a better life. These included:

- Job Opportunities: The North experienced rapid industrialization and urbanization during the late 19th and early 20th centuries, creating a high demand for labor in factories, mills, and other industries. African Americans saw the North as a place where they could find employment and economic security unavailable to them in the South.

- Promise of Freedom and Equality: The North was perceived as a place where African Americans could escape the oppressive racial hierarchies of the South and enjoy greater freedom and equality. Although racism and discrimination were still prevalent in the North, African Americans believed that they would have more opportunities to assert their rights and pursue their aspirations in Northern cities.

- Community and Culture: Northern cities like Chicago, New York, and Philadelphia offered vibrant African American communities where migrants could find solidarity, support, and cultural enrichment. Churches, social clubs, and cultural institutions provided spaces for African Americans to come together, celebrate their heritage, and organize for social and political change.

In the chapters that follow, we will explore the journey of African Americans as they embarked on the Great Migration, leaving behind the familiar but oppressive conditions of the South in search of a better future in the North. Through their stories, we will gain insight into the profound impact of the Great Migration on American society and culture, and the enduring legacy of this historic movement.

Chapter 2: Roots of Oppression

The roots of African American oppression in the United States run deep, tracing back to the institution of slavery and its enduring legacy in the post-Civil War South. In this chapter, we will explore the historical context of slavery and its lasting impact on African American communities, as well as the implementation of Jim Crow laws and systemic racism that perpetuated oppression in the South.

Section 1: The Legacy of Slavery

Slavery in the United States was a brutal and dehumanizing institution that persisted for over two centuries, shaping the social, economic, and political landscape of the nation. African slaves were forcibly brought to the American colonies beginning in the 17th century, where they were subjected to inhumane treatment, exploitation, and forced labor.

1.1 Origins of American Slavery

The institution of slavery in America had its roots in the transatlantic slave trade, in which millions of Africans were forcibly captured and transported to the Americas to work on plantations and in other industries. Slavery became deeply entrenched in the Southern colonies, where it provided the labor force necessary for the cultivation of crops such as tobacco, rice, and later, cotton.

1.2 Impact of Slavery on African American Communities

Slavery had a profound and lasting impact on African American communities, both during and after its abolition. Enslaved Africans were stripped of their humanity, their freedom, and their dignity, subjected to violence, exploitation, and degradation. Families were torn apart as individuals were bought and sold like property, and cultural ties were severed as African languages, religions, and traditions were suppressed.

1.3 Aftermath of Emancipation

The end of slavery with the Emancipation Proclamation in 1863 and the ratification of the 13th Amendment in 1865 marked a new chapter in African American history. However, the legacy of slavery endured long after its formal abolition, as African Americans continued to face discrimination, oppression, and violence in the post-Civil War South.

Section 2: Rise of Jim Crow Laws

In the decades following the Civil War, white Southerners sought to maintain their dominance and control over African Americans through the implementation of Jim Crow laws. Named after a minstrel character that portrayed African Americans in a derogatory manner, Jim Crow laws enforced racial segregation and discrimination, effectively creating a system of apartheid in the South.

2.1 Legalized Segregation

Jim Crow laws mandated the separation of public facilities, including schools, transportation, restaurants, and even drinking fountains, based on race. African Americans were relegated to inferior facilities and denied access to basic services and amenities that were reserved for whites. Segregation extended to all aspects of life, perpetuating a strict racial hierarchy and reinforcing white supremacy.

2.2 Systemic Racism and Violence

Beyond segregation, Jim Crow laws were enforced through systemic racism and violence, with African Americans facing harassment, intimidation, and even lynching for daring to challenge the status quo. The Ku Klux Klan and other white supremacist organizations terrorized African American communities, perpetuating a climate of fear and intimidation that further marginalized African Americans.

2.3 Economic Exploitation

In addition to legal segregation and violence, African Americans in the South were subjected to economic exploitation and disenfranchisement. Sharecropping and tenant farming replaced slavery as the dominant economic system, trapping African American farmers in a cycle of debt and poverty. Discriminatory labor practices and wage disparities further perpetuated economic inequality and social immobility.

Section 3: Resistance and Resilience

Despite the oppressive conditions of slavery, Jim Crow laws, and systemic racism, African Americans in the South demonstrated remarkable resilience and resistance in the face of adversity. From the abolitionist movements of the 19th century to the civil rights struggles of the 20th century, African Americans fought tirelessly for freedom, equality, and justice.

3.1 Abolitionist Movements

Throughout the antebellum period, African Americans and their allies organized abolitionist movements to challenge the institution of slavery and advocate for emancipation. Figures such as Frederick Douglass, Harriet Tubman, and Sojourner Truth played key roles in the abolitionist movement, using their voices and their actions to inspire change and mobilize support for the cause of freedom.

3.2 Civil Rights Struggles

The fight for civil rights continued into the 20th century, as African Americans confronted the injustices of segregation, discrimination, and disenfranchisement in the South. The NAACP, founded in 1909, became a leading voice for civil rights, advocating for legal challenges to segregation and mobilizing grassroots movements for social and political change.

3.3 Legacy of Resistance

The legacy of resistance and resilience in the face of oppression continues to inspire and empower African American communities today. From the Civil Rights Movement to the Black Lives Matter movement, African Americans have continued to fight for equality, justice, and dignity, challenging systemic racism and working towards a more inclusive and equitable society.

In the chapters that follow, we will explore the impact of slavery, Jim Crow laws, and systemic racism on African American communities in the South, as well as the migration of African Americans to the North in search of freedom, opportunity, and a better life. Through their stories, we will gain a deeper understanding of the enduring legacy of African American oppression and the ongoing struggle for liberation and justice.

Chapter 3: The Promise of the North

The early 20th century saw a dramatic shift in the economic landscape of the United States, as industrialization transformed Northern cities into centers of opportunity and prosperity. For African Americans fleeing the oppressive conditions of the South, the North represented a promise of economic advancement, social mobility, and freedom from racial discrimination. In this chapter, we will explore the economic opportunities that drew African Americans to Northern cities during this period and the rise of industrialization that fueled the demand for labor in urban centers.

Section 1: Economic Transformation

The late 19th and early 20th centuries witnessed a period of rapid industrialization in the United States, characterized by technological innovation, urbanization, and the growth of manufacturing industries. Northern cities such as Chicago, New York, Detroit, and Philadelphia emerged as industrial powerhouses, attracting millions of migrants from rural areas and foreign countries in search of employment and opportunity.

1.1 Rise of Manufacturing

The manufacturing sector played a central role in the economic transformation of the North, as factories and mills sprung up across urban centers, producing goods ranging from textiles and machinery to automobiles and steel. Advancements in transportation, communication, and infrastructure facilitated the expansion of industry, while government policies and investments encouraged entrepreneurship and innovation.

1.2 Urbanization and Population Growth

As industries flourished, Northern cities experienced unprecedented population growth and urbanization. Immigrants from Europe and migrants from rural areas flocked to urban centers in search of work, swelling the ranks of factory workers, laborers, and service workers. Cities expanded rapidly, with new neighborhoods, tenement buildings, and industrial districts springing up to accommodate the influx of newcomers.

1.3 Diversification of the Economy

The economic boom of the early 20th century led to a diversification of the Northern economy, as new industries emerged and existing industries expanded.

Alongside traditional manufacturing sectors such as textiles and steel, industries such as automobile manufacturing, electronics, and consumer goods production experienced rapid growth, creating a wide range of job opportunities for workers with diverse skills and backgrounds.

Section 2: Demand for Labor

The expansion of industry in the North created a high demand for labor, as factories, mills, and other businesses sought to meet growing production demands and capitalize on new market opportunities. African Americans, who had long been relegated to low-wage agricultural labor in the South, were drawn to the North by the promise of better-paying jobs and greater economic security.

2.1 Recruitment of African American Workers

Northern industries actively recruited African American workers to fill labor shortages and meet production quotas. Labor agents and recruiters traveled to the South, promising higher wages, better working conditions, and freedom from racial discrimination to entice African Americans to make the journey North. Many African Americans saw migration as a means of escaping the economic hardships and racial violence of the South and pursuing a better life for themselves and their families.

2.2 Role of the Great Migration

The Great Migration of African Americans from the South to the North, which began in earnest during the early 20th century and continued for several decades, played a pivotal role in meeting the labor demands of Northern industries. Millions of African Americans made the journey North, settling in cities such as Chicago, Detroit, Cleveland, and New York, where they found employment in factories, meatpacking plants, foundries, and other industrial enterprises.

2.3 Impact on Urban Development

The influx of African American migrants had a profound impact on the social, cultural, and economic fabric of Northern cities. Neighborhoods such as Chicago's Bronzeville, Detroit's Black Bottom, and Harlem in New York became vibrant hubs of African American culture and community, characterized by thriving businesses, churches, social clubs, and cultural institutions. Despite facing racial discrimination and segregation, African Americans in the North forged tight-knit communities and built networks of support that enabled them to navigate the challenges of urban life and pursue their aspirations for economic advancement and social mobility.

Section 3: Challenges and Opportunities

While the North offered greater economic opportunities and freedoms than the South, African Americans still faced significant challenges and obstacles in their quest for a better life. Discrimination, segregation, and racial violence persisted in Northern cities, limiting African Americans' access to housing, education, and employment opportunities. However, despite these challenges, many African Americans found ways to thrive and succeed in the North, building businesses, advancing their careers, and contributing to the cultural and economic vitality of their communities.

3.1 Housing Discrimination

One of the most pressing challenges facing African Americans in the North was housing discrimination, as restrictive covenants, redlining, and racially motivated violence prevented African Americans from accessing quality housing in desirable neighborhoods. Many African Americans were forced to live in overcrowded tenements, slums, and segregated housing projects, where they faced substandard living conditions, overcrowding, and limited access to basic services and amenities.

3.2 Employment Discrimination

African Americans in the North also faced discrimination and barriers to employment, as employers often favored white workers over African American workers for skilled and supervisory positions. African American workers were often relegated to low-wage, low-skilled jobs in industries such as domestic service, janitorial work, and unskilled labor, where they faced exploitation, discrimination, and limited opportunities for advancement.

3.3 Social and Cultural Resistance

Despite facing discrimination and segregation, African Americans in the North engaged in social and cultural resistance, challenging the status quo and advocating for civil rights and equality. Organizations such as the NAACP, the Urban League, and the Brotherhood of Sleeping Car Porters fought tirelessly for racial justice, organizing boycotts, protests, and legal challenges to combat discrimination and segregation in housing, employment, education, and public accommodations.

In the chapters that follow, we will explore the experiences of African Americans in Northern cities during the early 20th century, examining the opportunities and challenges they faced as they pursued economic advancement, social mobility, and freedom from racial oppression. Through their stories, we will gain insight into the complex dynamics of race, class, and power in urban America and the enduring legacy of the Great Migration on African American communities and culture.

Chapter 4: Exodus Begins

The Great Migration of African Americans from the South to the North began as a trickle in the late 19th century but soon swelled into a mass movement of people seeking refuge from the oppressive conditions of the Jim Crow South and the promise of economic opportunity and freedom in the North. In this chapter, we will explore the early signs of migration, the stories of individuals and families who embarked on the journey North, and the challenges and risks they faced along the way.

Section 1: Seeds of Migration

The seeds of the Great Migration were planted in the aftermath of the Civil War, as African Americans sought to escape the economic hardships, racial violence, and political disenfranchisement of the post-Reconstruction South. While the majority of African Americans remained in the South in the decades following Emancipation, a small but steady stream of migrants began to make their way North in search of a better life.

1.1 Push Factors

Several factors pushed African Americans to leave the South and venture North. Economic opportunities were limited in the agricultural South, where sharecropping and tenant farming kept African Americans trapped in a cycle of poverty and debt. Racial violence and discrimination also drove many African Americans to seek refuge in the North, where they hoped to find greater safety and freedom from persecution.

1.2 Pull Factors

At the same time, the North offered a number of attractions that drew African Americans seeking a better life. The promise of higher wages, better working conditions, and greater opportunities for social and economic advancement lured migrants to cities such as Chicago, Detroit, New York, and Philadelphia. The presence of established African American communities in Northern cities provided newcomers with a sense of solidarity and support as they embarked on their journey North.

Section 2: Stories of Migration

The Great Migration was driven by the individual decisions of millions of African Americans who chose to leave the South and seek their fortunes in the

North. Their stories are as varied as the people themselves, reflecting the diverse motivations, experiences, and challenges faced by migrants during this period.

2.1 Economic Opportunity

For many migrants, the decision to leave the South was driven by economic necessity. Sharecroppers and tenant farmers struggling to make ends meet saw migration as a chance to escape the cycle of debt and poverty that plagued rural life in the South. Others were drawn by the promise of higher wages and better job opportunities in the North, where industries such as manufacturing, transportation, and construction were booming.

2.2 Escape from Violence and Oppression

Racial violence and discrimination were pervasive in the Jim Crow South, driving many African Americans to seek refuge in the North. Lynchings, mob attacks, and other acts of racial terror targeted African Americans who dared to challenge the status quo or assert their rights. Fleeing to the North offered migrants the hope of escaping the constant threat of violence and finding a measure of safety and security for themselves and their families.

2.3 Search for Freedom and Equality

The promise of freedom and equality in the North also motivated many migrants to leave the South. Despite the legal end of slavery with the Emancipation Proclamation and the ratification of the 13th Amendment, African Americans in the South continued to face systemic racism and oppression under Jim Crow laws. Migration offered African Americans the chance to escape the rigid racial hierarchy of the South and assert their rights as free citizens in the North.

Section 3: Challenges and Risks

While migration offered the promise of a better life, it also entailed significant risks and challenges for African Americans leaving the South. The journey North was fraught with obstacles, from the physical dangers of travel to the social and economic challenges of settling in a new and unfamiliar environment.

3.1 Physical Hazards

Traveling from the South to the North was no easy feat, particularly for African Americans who lacked access to reliable transportation and faced discrimination and violence along the way. Many migrants traveled by train, bus, or even on foot, enduring long and arduous journeys that could take days or even weeks to complete. Along the way, they faced the risk of robbery, assault, and other dangers posed by unscrupulous individuals and hostile communities.

3.2 Social and Economic Challenges

Settling in the North presented its own set of challenges for migrants, from finding housing and employment to navigating unfamiliar social and cultural landscapes. Housing discrimination and segregation limited African Americans' access to quality housing in desirable neighborhoods, forcing many migrants to live in overcrowded tenements and slums. Employment discrimination and wage disparities also made it difficult for African Americans to find stable and well-paying jobs, despite the high demand for labor in Northern industries.

3.3 Psychological and Emotional Strain

The journey North took a toll on migrants' physical and emotional well-being, as they grappled with the uncertainty and upheaval of leaving behind their homes, families, and communities. Many migrants experienced feelings of isolation, homesickness, and alienation as they struggled to adapt to their new surroundings and forge connections in unfamiliar cities. The loss of familiar landmarks, traditions, and support networks compounded the psychological strain of migration, leaving many migrants feeling adrift and disconnected from their roots.

Despite these challenges and risks, millions of African Americans made the journey North in search of a better life, driven by a powerful desire for freedom, opportunity, and equality. Their courage, resilience, and determination laid the foundation for the Great Migration, shaping the destinies of individuals, families, and communities for generations to come.

Chapter 5: Chicago: The New Promised Land

Among the many destinations for African American migrants during the Great Migration, Chicago emerged as one of the primary magnets, drawing thousands of individuals and families seeking refuge from the oppressive conditions of the South and the promise of economic opportunity and social mobility in the North. In this chapter, we will explore the appeal of Chicago for African American migrants, the formation of vibrant communities such as Bronzeville, and the enduring legacy of African American presence in the city.

Section 1: Chicago: The Promised Land

Chicago's rise as a destination for African American migrants during the Great Migration was fueled by a combination of factors, including its booming economy, its central location in the Midwest, and its reputation as a bastion of freedom and opportunity for African Americans fleeing the Jim Crow South. The city's position as a transportation hub and its diverse industrial base made it an attractive destination for migrants seeking employment in factories, meatpacking plants, and other industries.

1.1 Economic Opportunity

Chicago's economy was booming in the early 20th century, fueled by the growth of manufacturing, transportation, and commerce. The city's meatpacking industry, centered around the Union Stockyards, provided thousands of jobs for African American migrants, who found employment as meatpackers, butchers, and laborers. Other industries, such as steel manufacturing, automobile production, and food processing, also offered opportunities for employment and economic advancement.

1.2 Central Location

Chicago's central location in the Midwest made it a natural gateway for African American migrants traveling from the South to the North. Situated at the crossroads of major transportation routes, including railroads and waterways, Chicago served as a transit hub for migrants making their way to Northern cities. The city's accessibility and proximity to other urban centers in the Midwest made it an attractive destination for migrants seeking refuge from the Jim Crow South.

1.3 Reputation for Opportunity

Chicago's reputation as a city of opportunity and freedom for African Americans grew as migrants began to settle in the city and build communities of their own. The presence of established African American neighborhoods, churches, and social institutions provided newcomers with a sense of belonging and support as they embarked on their journey North. Word of mouth and personal networks also played a role in attracting migrants to Chicago, as individuals and families shared their experiences and success stories with friends and relatives back home.

Section 2: Formation of Bronzeville

One of the most vibrant and iconic African American communities to emerge in Chicago during the Great Migration was Bronzeville, located on the city's South Side. Formed by migrants from the South and immigrants from the Caribbean, Bronzeville became a cultural and economic center for African Americans in Chicago, offering a sense of community, pride, and resilience in the face of adversity.

2.1 Early Settlement

African American settlement in Bronzeville began in the late 19th century, as migrants from the South and immigrants from the Caribbean began to arrive in Chicago in search of employment and opportunity. Initially confined to segregated areas of the city, African Americans gradually began to establish their presence in neighborhoods such as Bronzeville, where they found affordable housing, job opportunities, and a supportive community network.

2.2 Cultural Renaissance

Bronzeville flourished during the early 20th century, becoming a vibrant hub of African American culture, art, and literature. The neighborhood was home to a thriving community of artists, musicians, writers, and intellectuals who contributed to the Harlem Renaissance and the broader cultural movements of the period. Jazz clubs, theaters, and literary salons proliferated in Bronzeville, providing spaces for African Americans to celebrate their heritage, express their creativity, and engage in intellectual exchange.

2.3 Economic Prosperity

Bronzeville was also a center of economic activity for African Americans in Chicago, with businesses ranging from barber shops and beauty salons to restaurants, grocery stores, and nightclubs. The neighborhood's main thoroughfare, known as the "Stroll," was lined with businesses owned and operated by African Americans, creating a vibrant commercial district that catered to the needs and interests of the community. African American entrepreneurs thrived in Bronzeville, building successful businesses and contributing to the economic vitality of the neighborhood.

2.4 Community Institutions

Bronzeville was home to a wide range of community institutions that provided essential services and support to residents. Churches played a central role in the social and spiritual life of the neighborhood, providing not only religious services but also educational, social, and cultural programs for members of the community. Schools, libraries, and community centers offered resources and opportunities for learning and enrichment, while social clubs, fraternal organizations, and mutual aid societies provided support and solidarity in times of need.

Section 3: Legacy of Bronzeville

While Bronzeville experienced periods of decline and disinvestment in the latter half of the 20th century, its legacy as a cultural and economic center for African Americans in Chicago endures to this day. The neighborhood's rich history and cultural heritage continue to be celebrated and preserved by residents and community organizations, who work to honor the contributions of past generations and ensure a bright future for the neighborhood.

3.1 Cultural Heritage

Bronzeville's cultural heritage is celebrated through a variety of festivals, events, and cultural institutions that showcase the neighborhood's history and artistic legacy. The Bronzeville Visitor Information Center, the Bronzeville Walk of Fame, and the DuSable Museum of African American History are just a few of the attractions that highlight Bronzeville's significance as a center of African American culture and creativity.

3.2 Economic Revitalization

In recent years, efforts have been underway to revitalize Bronzeville's economy and attract investment to the neighborhood. Community organizations, business owners, and local government officials have collaborated on initiatives to promote economic development, create jobs, and improve the quality of life for residents. Projects such as the redevelopment of vacant lots and abandoned buildings, the expansion of affordable housing options, and the promotion of small business entrepreneurship are helping to bring new life and opportunity to Bronzeville.

3.3 Social Justice and Equity

Bronzeville's legacy of resilience and resistance is reflected in ongoing efforts to address social justice and equity issues in the neighborhood and beyond. Community activists, organizers, and leaders are working to combat systemic racism, poverty, and inequality, advocating for policies and programs that promote economic opportunity, social justice, and racial equity. Through their collective efforts, residents of Bronzeville are continuing to build on the legacy of past generations and create a more inclusive and equitable future for their community and city.

In the chapters that follow, we will explore the experiences of African Americans in other Northern cities during the Great Migration, examining the formation of vibrant communities and the enduring legacy of African American presence in urban America. Through their stories, we will gain insight into the complex dynamics of race, class, and power in Northern cities and the ongoing struggle for justice, equality, and opportunity for all.

Chapter 6: Harlem Renaissance and Cultural Awakening

The Great Migration of African Americans from the South to the North during the early 20th century not only transformed the demographic landscape of urban America but also gave rise to a vibrant cultural movement known as the Harlem Renaissance. This period of artistic, literary, and intellectual flourishing in the predominantly African American neighborhood of Harlem, New York, became a symbol of cultural rebirth and creativity for African Americans across the nation. In this chapter, we will explore the impact of the Great Migration on African American arts, literature, and culture, and examine the Harlem Renaissance as a pivotal moment in American history.

Section 1: The Great Migration and Cultural Transformation

The Great Migration brought millions of African Americans to Northern cities like New York, Chicago, and Detroit, where they encountered new opportunities, challenges, and experiences. The migration not only reshaped the demographic landscape of urban America but also catalyzed a cultural transformation, as African Americans brought their rich heritage, traditions, and experiences with them to their new homes in the North.

1.1 Migration and Urbanization

The influx of African American migrants to Northern cities during the Great Migration fueled the growth of vibrant, diverse communities that became hubs of cultural exchange and creativity. Neighborhoods such as Harlem in New York, Bronzeville in Chicago, and Paradise Valley in Detroit became centers of African American culture, where migrants found solidarity, support, and inspiration as they navigated the challenges of urban life.

1.2 Cultural Exchange and Fusion

The Great Migration facilitated a rich exchange of cultural traditions, ideas, and influences among African Americans from different regions and backgrounds. In Northern cities, migrants encountered new styles of music, art, literature, and performance, as well as diverse cultural practices and customs from African, Caribbean, and European traditions. This cultural fusion and hybridity gave rise to new forms of expression and creativity that reflected the unique experiences and perspectives of African Americans in the urban North.

1.3 Creative Expression and Identity

The Great Migration provided African American artists, writers, musicians, and intellectuals with new opportunities to express themselves and explore their identities in ways that were not possible in the racially segregated South. Freed from the constraints of Jim Crow laws and social norms, African American creatives embraced their cultural heritage and celebrated their identity through their work, contributing to a burgeoning cultural renaissance that reshaped American art, literature, and music.

Section 2: The Harlem Renaissance

The Harlem Renaissance was a cultural and intellectual movement that emerged in the 1920s and 1930s in the predominantly African American neighborhood of Harlem, New York. It was characterized by a surge of creativity and innovation in literature, music, visual arts, theater, and dance, as African American artists, writers, and intellectuals sought to challenge stereotypes, redefine racial identity, and assert their cultural and political autonomy.

2.1 Literary Renaissance

The Harlem Renaissance produced a wealth of literature that captured the vibrancy and complexity of African American life in the urban North. Writers such as Langston Hughes, Zora Neale Hurston, Claude McKay, and Jean Toomer explored themes of race, identity, migration, and social justice in their poetry, novels, essays, and short stories, challenging prevailing stereotypes and prejudices and offering new perspectives on the African American experience.

2.2 Visual Arts and Expressionism

The Harlem Renaissance also witnessed a flourishing of visual arts and expressionism, as African American artists explored themes of identity, history, and culture through painting, sculpture, photography, and mixed media. Artists such as Aaron Douglas, Jacob Lawrence, Romare Bearden, and Augusta Savage drew inspiration from African art, jazz music, and social activism, creating powerful and evocative works that reflected the spirit of the times and the struggles and triumphs of African American life.

2.3 Music and Jazz Age

Music played a central role in the Harlem Renaissance, with jazz emerging as the soundtrack of the era. Jazz clubs such as the Cotton Club, the Savoy Ballroom, and the Apollo Theater became iconic venues where African American musicians, singers, and dancers showcased their talent and creativity, contributing to the development of new styles and genres that revolutionized American music and popular culture. Musicians such as Duke Ellington, Louis Armstrong, Bessie Smith, and Billie Holiday became household names, captivating audiences with their virtuosity, innovation, and emotional depth.

Section 3: Legacy of the Harlem Renaissance

The legacy of the Harlem Renaissance extends far beyond the 1920s and 1930s, shaping the course of American culture and society in profound and lasting ways. The movement not only transformed African American arts, literature, and culture but also challenged prevailing notions of race, identity, and representation, paving the way for future generations of artists, writers, and activists to continue the struggle for social justice and equality.

3.1 Cultural Influence and Impact

The Harlem Renaissance left an indelible mark on American culture, influencing artistic movements such as the Civil Rights Movement, the Black Arts Movement, and the Hip-Hop movement, as well as popular culture, fashion, and design. The works of Harlem Renaissance artists and writers continue to be studied, celebrated, and admired for their innovation, creativity, and social relevance, inspiring new generations of creators and thinkers to explore the complexities of the African American experience.

3.2 Political and Social Legacy

The Harlem Renaissance was not just a cultural movement but also a political and social one, as African American artists, writers, and intellectuals used their platforms to advocate for racial justice, civil rights, and social change. Through their art, literature, and activism, Harlem Renaissance figures challenged the prevailing racial hierarchy and demanded recognition, respect, and equality for African Americans in American society.

3.3 Celebration and Remembrance

Today, the Harlem Renaissance is celebrated and remembered through a variety of cultural institutions, events, and initiatives that honor its legacy and contributions to American history and culture. Museums such as the Studio Museum in Harlem, the Schomburg Center for Research in Black Culture, and the National Museum of African American History and Culture preserve and showcase the art, literature, and artifacts of the Harlem Renaissance, ensuring that its legacy continues to inspire and educate future generations.

In the chapters that follow, we will explore the impact of the Great Migration and the Harlem Renaissance on other aspects of American society and culture, examining the enduring legacy of African American presence in urban America and the ongoing struggle for justice, equality, and opportunity for all.

Chapter 7: Urban Challenges

The Great Migration brought millions of African Americans from the rural South to the urban North in search of economic opportunity, social mobility, and freedom from racial oppression. However, the transition from rural to urban life presented a myriad of challenges for migrants, as they grappled with issues such as housing discrimination, overcrowding, poverty, and social isolation. In this chapter, we will explore the struggles faced by migrants in adapting to urban life in Northern cities and the systemic barriers that perpetuated inequality and injustice.

Section 1: The Transition to Urban Life

For many African American migrants, the move from the rural South to the urban North represented a profound shift in lifestyle, culture, and identity. Accustomed to the rhythms of rural life, migrants found themselves thrust into the bustling, fast-paced world of the city, where they encountered new challenges and opportunities.

1.1 Cultural Adjustment

The transition to urban life required migrants to adapt to unfamiliar customs, social norms, and modes of behavior. Many migrants faced culture shock as they navigated the complexities of urban society, grappling with issues such as language barriers, unfamiliar social hierarchies, and the loss of familiar community ties. For those who had spent their entire lives in rural areas, the sights, sounds, and smells of the city could be overwhelming, leading to feelings of disorientation and alienation.

1.2 Economic Struggles

While the North offered greater economic opportunities than the South, many migrants found themselves struggling to make ends meet in the competitive urban environment. Jobs were often scarce, wages were low, and employment discrimination was rampant, particularly for African Americans who lacked education, skills, or social connections. As a result, many migrants were forced to take on low-paying, insecure jobs in industries such as domestic service, janitorial work, and unskilled labor, where they faced exploitation, discrimination, and limited opportunities for advancement.

1.3 Social Isolation

The anonymity of urban life could be isolating for migrants who found themselves far from the familiar comforts of home and family. In the crowded tenements and apartment buildings of Northern cities, neighbors were often strangers, and community ties were fragmented by the transient nature of urban life. Social isolation and loneliness were common experiences for migrants who struggled to find connections and support networks in their new surroundings.

Section 2: Housing Discrimination and Segregation

One of the most pressing challenges faced by African American migrants in Northern cities was housing discrimination and segregation, which limited their access to quality housing and perpetuated racial inequality and injustice.

2.1 Restrictive Covenants

Housing discrimination was institutionalized through the use of restrictive covenants, which were clauses inserted into property deeds that prohibited the sale or rental of real estate to African Americans and other minority groups. These covenants effectively segregated residential neighborhoods along racial lines, confining African Americans to overcrowded, substandard housing in segregated ghettos and slums.

2.2 Redlining

Redlining, a practice used by banks and mortgage lenders to deny loans and financial services to residents of predominantly African American neighborhoods, further entrenched housing segregation and discrimination. By labeling African American communities as "high-risk" or "undesirable," lenders effectively denied residents access to the capital needed to purchase or improve their homes, perpetuating cycles of poverty and disinvestment in African American neighborhoods.

2.3 Housing Conditions

For African American migrants living in Northern cities, housing conditions were often deplorable, characterized by overcrowding, substandard construction, and lack of basic amenities. Tenement buildings, which housed multiple families in cramped, unsanitary conditions, were common in African American neighborhoods, where landlords exploited tenants and neglected maintenance and repairs. Many migrants lived in dilapidated housing with inadequate heating, plumbing, and ventilation, exposing them to health risks and environmental hazards.

Section 3: Poverty and Inequality

The Great Migration promised economic opportunity and social mobility for African American migrants, but for many, the reality was far from the American dream. Poverty and inequality were pervasive in Northern cities, where African Americans faced systemic barriers to economic advancement and social inclusion.

3.1 Economic Exploitation

African American migrants in Northern cities were often relegated to the lowest-paying, least desirable jobs in the labor market, where they faced exploitation, discrimination, and limited opportunities for advancement. Jobs in industries such as domestic service, janitorial work, and unskilled labor offered low wages, few benefits, and little job security, trapping workers in a cycle of poverty and economic dependency.

3.2 Wage Disparities

Despite their contributions to the economic prosperity of Northern cities, African American workers were systematically underpaid and undervalued compared to their white counterparts. Wage disparities based on race and ethnicity were common in industries such as manufacturing, construction, and service, where African American workers were often paid less than white workers for the same work or denied access to higher-paying positions and opportunities for advancement.

3.3 Lack of Social Services

The social safety net in Northern cities was woefully inadequate to meet the needs of African American migrants struggling to make ends meet. Public services and amenities such as schools, hospitals, parks, and public transportation were often segregated and underfunded in African American neighborhoods, depriving residents of access to quality education, healthcare, and recreational opportunities. Social welfare programs such as public housing, food assistance, and unemployment insurance were limited in scope and availability, leaving many migrants vulnerable to poverty, homelessness, and social exclusion.

Section 4: Resilience and Resistance

Despite the myriad challenges faced by African American migrants in Northern cities, they demonstrated remarkable resilience and resistance in the face of adversity. From organizing labor unions and community organizations to advocating for civil rights and social justice, African Americans in the North fought tirelessly for equality, dignity, and opportunity for themselves and future generations.

4.1 Community Organizing

African American migrants in Northern cities organized grassroots movements and community organizations to address the social, economic, and political challenges facing their communities. From tenant unions and neighborhood associations to civil rights groups and mutual aid societies, these organizations provided a platform for collective action and empowerment, enabling residents to mobilize resources, build solidarity, and advocate for change.

4.2 Civil Rights Activism

The struggle for civil rights and racial justice was central to African American life in Northern cities, where migrants confronted systemic racism and discrimination in housing, employment, education, and public accommodations. Organizations such as the NAACP, the Urban League, and the Congress of Racial Equality (CORE) led campaigns for desegregation, fair housing, and equal employment opportunities, organizing protests, boycotts, and legal challenges to challenge the status quo and advance the cause of civil rights.

4.3 Cultural Resistance

African American artists, writers, musicians, and intellectuals played a vital role in the struggle for social justice and equality, using their creative talents and platforms to challenge stereotypes, inspire activism, and promote cultural pride and identity. From the Harlem Renaissance to the Black Arts Movement, African American cultural movements have served as vehicles for resistance, resilience, and transformation, empowering individuals and communities to assert their voices, celebrate their heritage, and demand recognition and respect in American society.

In the chapters that follow, we will explore the impact of the Great Migration and urbanization on other aspects of American society and culture, examining the enduring legacy of African American presence in urban America and the ongoing struggle for justice, equality, and opportunity for all.

Chapter 8: Rise of the Civil Rights Movement

The Great Migration played a pivotal role in shaping the early Civil Rights Movement in the United States, catalyzing a wave of activism and resistance against racial segregation and discrimination. As African Americans migrated from the rural South to the urban North in search of economic opportunity and social justice, they brought with them a deep sense of determination, resilience, and commitment to challenging the status quo and fighting for equality and civil rights. In this chapter, we will explore the role of migration in shaping the early Civil Rights Movement and the grassroots activism and resistance efforts that emerged in response to racial segregation and discrimination.

Section 1: Seeds of Change

The seeds of the Civil Rights Movement were sown long before the Great Migration, as African Americans in the South and North alike fought tirelessly for freedom, justice, and equality in the face of entrenched racism and oppression. However, the mass migration of African Americans from the rural South to the urban North during the early 20th century brought new energy, resources, and perspectives to the struggle for civil rights, laying the groundwork for the transformative social movements that would follow.

1.1 Migration and Consciousness

The Great Migration was a transformative experience for African American migrants, many of whom had grown up in the Jim Crow South and experienced firsthand the brutality of racial segregation and discrimination. The move to the North exposed migrants to new ideas, opportunities, and possibilities, opening their eyes to the possibility of a different future and inspiring them to take action to challenge the status quo and demand change.

1.2 Urban Centers of Activism

Northern cities such as Chicago, New York, Detroit, and Philadelphia became centers of African American activism and resistance during the early 20th century, as migrants organized grassroots movements and community organizations to address the social, economic, and political challenges facing their communities. From tenant unions and neighborhood associations to civil rights groups and mutual aid societies, these organizations provided a platform for collective action and empowerment, enabling residents to mobilize resources, build solidarity, and advocate for change.

1.3 Intersection of Movements

The Civil Rights Movement was deeply interconnected with other social justice movements of the time, including labor rights, women's rights, and immigrant rights. African American migrants played a central role in these movements, forming alliances and coalitions with other marginalized groups to advance common goals and objectives. From the labor strikes of the 1920s and 1930s to the campaigns for women's suffrage and immigrant rights, African American activists worked tirelessly to build bridges across racial, ethnic, and class lines and forge a more inclusive and equitable society for all.

Section 2: Grassroots Activism

The early Civil Rights Movement was characterized by grassroots activism and resistance efforts that challenged racial segregation and discrimination at the local level. From boycotts and sit-ins to marches and demonstrations, African American activists employed a variety of tactics and strategies to confront injustice, mobilize public opinion, and demand change.

2.1 Boycotts and Economic Pressure

Boycotts were a common tactic used by African American activists to challenge racial segregation and discrimination in Northern cities. By refusing to patronize businesses that practiced discrimination or supported segregationist policies, African American consumers and community members exerted economic pressure on businesses and institutions to change their practices and policies. Boycotts targeted a wide range of businesses, including restaurants, stores, theaters, and public transportation companies, and were often successful in achieving their goals.

2.2 Sit-Ins and Direct Action

Sit-ins and direct action campaigns were another powerful tool used by African American activists to challenge racial segregation and discrimination in public spaces. Sit-ins involved occupying segregated facilities such as lunch counters, restaurants, and theaters to protest segregationist policies and demand equal treatment and access. These nonviolent protests drew national attention to the issue of racial injustice and inspired similar actions in other cities, helping to build momentum for the broader Civil Rights Movement.

2.3 Legal Challenges and Litigation

Legal challenges and litigation were an important component of the early Civil Rights Movement, as African American activists used the courts to challenge segregationist laws and practices and secure legal protections for their rights. Organizations such as the NAACP and the ACLU played a leading role in bringing lawsuits and test cases to challenge segregation in education, housing, employment, and public accommodations, laying the groundwork for landmark Supreme Court decisions such as Brown v. Board of Education and Shelley v. Kraemer.

Section 3: Resistance and Repression

The rise of the Civil Rights Movement met with fierce resistance and repression from defenders of the status quo, who sought to maintain white supremacy and preserve racial segregation and discrimination at all costs. African American activists and their allies faced harassment, intimidation, violence, and legal persecution as they fought for their rights and demanded justice and equality.

3.1 White Resistance

White resistance to the Civil Rights Movement took many forms, from overt acts of violence and terror to more subtle forms of discrimination and exclusion. Segregationists and white supremacists organized vigilante groups such as the Ku Klux Klan to intimidate and terrorize African American activists and their supporters, while politicians and policymakers enacted laws and policies to maintain racial segregation and uphold white privilege and power.

3.2 State Violence

State and local authorities often colluded with white supremacists to suppress the Civil Rights Movement through violence, intimidation, and legal repression. Police brutality, mass arrests, and wrongful convictions were common tactics used to quell protests and demonstrations, while government agencies such as the FBI and the CIA engaged in surveillance, infiltration, and disruption of civil rights organizations and leaders. The murders of civil rights activists such as Medgar Evers, Emmett Till, and Viola Liuzzo served as grim reminders of the dangers faced by those who dared to challenge the racial status quo.

3.3 Resilience and Resistance

Despite the repression and violence they faced, African American activists remained resilient and determined in their struggle for justice and equality. They continued to organize, mobilize, and resist, refusing to be silenced or intimidated by the forces of oppression. Their courage, resilience, and sacrifice inspired millions of Americans to join the fight for civil rights and helped to galvanize support for the broader Civil Rights Movement.

In the chapters that follow, we will explore the continuing impact of the Great Migration and the Civil Rights Movement on American society and culture, examining the enduring legacy of African American activism and resistance and the ongoing struggle for justice, equality, and opportunity for all.

Chapter 9: Red Summer and Racial Tensions

The Great Migration of African Americans from the rural South to the urban North during the early 20th century brought with it a wave of escalating racial tensions and violence in Northern cities. The culmination of these tensions exploded in the summer of 1919, a period now known as the Red Summer, during which widespread riots and racial violence swept across the country. In this chapter, we will explore the factors contributing to escalating racial tensions in Northern cities and the events of the Red Summer, as well as the lasting impact of this period on race relations in America.

Section 1: The Context of Racial Tensions

The Great Migration fundamentally altered the demographic landscape of Northern cities, as African Americans migrated in search of economic opportunity and escape from the oppressive conditions of the Jim Crow South. However, their arrival in Northern cities was met with hostility, resentment, and discrimination from both white residents and local authorities, fueling a climate of racial tension and animosity.

1.1 Economic Competition

African American migrants often found themselves competing with white residents for jobs, housing, and resources in Northern cities, leading to resentment and hostility from white workers and homeowners who viewed them as competitors and threats to their economic livelihoods. Labor unions and employers exploited racial divisions to undermine solidarity and maintain control over the workforce, exacerbating racial tensions and perpetuating inequality and discrimination in the workplace.

1.2 Housing Segregation

Segregated housing policies and practices further exacerbated racial tensions in Northern cities, as African American migrants were confined to overcrowded, substandard housing in segregated ghettos and slums, while white residents enjoyed access to better quality housing and neighborhoods. Housing discrimination, redlining, and restrictive covenants restricted African American access to homeownership and rental housing in desirable areas, perpetuating cycles of poverty, segregation, and inequality.

1.3 Police Brutality and Discrimination

Police brutality and discrimination against African Americans were widespread in Northern cities, as law enforcement agencies enforced racial segregation and maintained social control through violence, intimidation, and harassment. African American communities were subjected to racial profiling, arbitrary arrests, and excessive use of force by police officers, leading to deep-seated mistrust and resentment towards law enforcement and the criminal justice system.

Section 2: The Red Summer of 1919

The Red Summer of 1919 was a period of widespread racial violence and unrest that swept across the United States, fueled by escalating racial tensions and resentment towards African American migrants in Northern cities. The riots and bloodshed that ensued exposed the deep-seated racism and prejudice that pervaded American society and underscored the urgent need for social and political change.

2.1 Chicago Race Riot

The Chicago Race Riot of 1919 was one of the deadliest and most destructive episodes of racial violence during the Red Summer, lasting for nearly a week and resulting in dozens of deaths, hundreds of injuries, and extensive property damage. The riot was sparked by a violent confrontation between white and African American beachgoers at an unofficial segregated beach on Lake Michigan, which escalated into widespread looting, arson, and mob violence in African American neighborhoods on the South Side of Chicago.

2.2 Washington D.C. Riot

The Washington D.C. Riot of 1919 was another significant outbreak of racial violence during the Red Summer, triggered by the alleged assault of a white woman by African American men. The riot lasted for several days and resulted in numerous deaths, injuries, and extensive property damage, as mobs of white residents attacked African American neighborhoods and businesses in retaliation for the perceived affront to white honor and supremacy.

2.3 Other Riots and Unrest

The Red Summer saw riots and racial violence erupt in cities across the country, including Philadelphia, Omaha, and Elaine, Arkansas, among others. In each case, the violence was fueled by a combination of economic competition, racial resentment, and white supremacist ideology, as white mobs targeted

African American communities and businesses in acts of racial terror and intimidation.

Section 3: Aftermath and Legacy

The Red Summer of 1919 left a lasting legacy on race relations in America, exposing the deep divisions and inequalities that persisted despite the promise of freedom and opportunity in the North. The riots and violence of the Red Summer served as a wake-up call to policymakers, activists, and ordinary citizens alike, highlighting the urgent need for social and political reform to address the root causes of racial injustice and inequality.

3.1 Political Response

In the aftermath of the Red Summer, there was a renewed sense of urgency and determination among African American activists and leaders to demand justice, equality, and civil rights. Organizations such as the NAACP and the Urban League redoubled their efforts to challenge racial segregation and discrimination through legal advocacy, community organizing, and public education, while political leaders and policymakers began to acknowledge the need for reforms to address the underlying causes of racial unrest and violence.

3.2 Cultural Impact

The Red Summer also had a profound impact on African American culture and identity, inspiring a new generation of artists, writers, and intellectuals to explore themes of racial identity, social justice, and resistance in their work. The riots and violence of the Red Summer were memorialized in literature, music, and art, serving as a powerful reminder of the struggles and sacrifices of African Americans in the fight for freedom and equality.

3.3 Continued Struggle

Despite the social and political reforms that followed in the wake of the Red Summer, racial tensions and inequality persisted in American society, as African Americans continued to face discrimination, segregation, and violence in Northern cities and beyond. The legacy of the Red Summer serves as a sobering reminder of the ongoing struggle for racial justice and equality in America, and the need for vigilance and solidarity in the face of injustice and oppression.

In the chapters that follow, we will continue to explore the impact of the Great Migration and the struggle for civil rights on American society and culture, examining the enduring legacy of African American activism and resistance and the ongoing quest for justice, equality, and opportunity for all.

Chapter 10: Economic Realities

The Great Migration of African Americans from the rural South to the urban North promised economic opportunity and social mobility, but the reality for many migrants was far from the American dream. In Northern cities, African Americans faced economic disparities, discrimination, and exploitation in the workplace, as they struggled to secure fair wages, decent working conditions, and opportunities for advancement. In this chapter, we will explore the economic realities faced by African Americans in the North and the grassroots efforts to fight for economic justice and equality.

Section 1: Economic Disparities

Despite the promise of economic opportunity, African Americans in Northern cities often found themselves marginalized and excluded from the mainstream economy, as they faced systemic barriers to employment, education, and economic advancement.

1.1 Employment Discrimination

African American migrants in the North encountered widespread employment discrimination, as employers and labor unions excluded them from skilled, high-paying jobs and relegated them to the lowest-paying, least desirable positions in the labor market. Discriminatory hiring practices, racial stereotypes, and segregated workplaces limited African American access to opportunities for advancement and perpetuated economic inequality and segregation in the workforce.

1.2 Occupational Segregation

Occupational segregation was a pervasive feature of the Northern labor market, as African Americans were disproportionately concentrated in low-wage, low-skilled industries such as domestic service, janitorial work, and unskilled labor. Segregated job markets and limited access to training and education opportunities further restricted African American mobility and economic prospects, trapping workers in low-paying, dead-end jobs with few opportunities for advancement or upward mobility.

1.3 Wage Disparities

Wage disparities based on race and ethnicity were endemic in Northern cities, as African American workers were systematically underpaid and undervalued compared to their white counterparts. African American workers earned significantly lower wages than white workers for the same work, and were often denied access to benefits, promotions, and opportunities for skill development and career advancement. Wage differentials perpetuated economic inequality and poverty in African American communities, limiting their ability to build wealth, achieve financial security, and improve their quality of life.

Section 2: Labor Exploitation

Labor exploitation was widespread in Northern industries such as manufacturing, agriculture, and service, as employers exploited African American workers for cheap labor and subjected them to unsafe working conditions, long hours, and low wages.

2.1 Industrial Labor

African American migrants were recruited to Northern cities to fill labor shortages in industries such as manufacturing, where they worked in factories, steel mills, and other industrial settings. However, African American workers were often relegated to the most dangerous, low-paying jobs on the assembly line, where they faced hazardous working conditions, exposure to toxic chemicals, and high rates of injury and death. Employers exploited African American labor for cheap, disposable workers, while denying them the rights and protections afforded to their white counterparts.

2.2 Agricultural Labor

Agricultural labor was another area of exploitation for African American workers in the North, as they toiled in fields, orchards, and vineyards under harsh conditions and for meager wages. African American farmworkers faced discrimination and exploitation from employers and landowners who profited from their labor while denying them fair wages, decent housing, and basic rights and protections. Many African American farmworkers were migrants from the rural South who had fled poverty and oppression, only to find themselves trapped in a cycle of exploitation and poverty in the North.

2.3 Service Labor

Service industries such as domestic work, janitorial services, and food service were major sources of employment for African American women in the North, who were often relegated to low-paying, insecure jobs with few benefits or protections. Domestic workers, in particular, faced exploitation and abuse from employers who took advantage of their vulnerability and lack of legal protections to extract maximum labor for minimum wages. Many African American women worked as domestic workers, janitors, and maids, performing essential but undervalued labor that sustained Northern households and industries.

Section 3: Fight for Fair Wages and Working Conditions

Despite the formidable obstacles they faced, African American workers in the North fought tirelessly for fair wages, decent working conditions, and economic justice, organizing labor unions, strikes, and protests to demand change and improve their lives.

3.1 Labor Organizing

Labor unions played a central role in the fight for economic justice and workers' rights in the North, as African American workers organized unions, strikes, and protests to challenge exploitation and discrimination in the workplace. Organizations such as the Brotherhood of Sleeping Car Porters, the National Negro Labor Council, and the Congress of Industrial Organizations (CIO) led campaigns for unionization and collective bargaining rights, mobilizing African American workers and allies to demand fair wages, safe working conditions, and dignity and respect on the job.

3.2 Strikes and Protests

Strikes and protests were powerful tools used by African American workers to assert their rights and demand change in the workplace. From the Brotherhood of Sleeping Car Porters' strike against the Pullman Company to the Detroit Race Riot of 1943, African American workers and communities mobilized to protest unfair labor practices, racial discrimination, and economic inequality, drawing attention to the plight of African American workers and galvanizing support for their cause.

3.3 Legal Advocacy

Legal advocacy and litigation were also important strategies used by African American workers to challenge exploitation and discrimination in the workplace. Organizations such as the NAACP and the ACLU brought lawsuits and legal challenges to challenge segregationist laws and practices, secure fair wages and working conditions, and protect workers' rights and freedoms. Landmark Supreme Court decisions such as Brown v. Board of Education and Shelley v. Kraemer paved the way for greater legal protections and opportunities for African American workers in the North.

In the chapters that follow, we will continue to explore the impact of the Great Migration and the struggle for economic justice on American society and culture, examining the enduring legacy of African American activism and resistance and the ongoing quest for equality, dignity, and opportunity for all.

Chapter 11: Women's Voices

The Great Migration of African Americans from the rural South to the urban North was not only a transformative experience for African American men but also for women, who played a vital role in shaping the social, cultural, and political landscape of Northern cities. In this chapter, we will explore the experiences of African American women during the Great Migration and the significant contributions they made to community building, activism, and social change.

Section 1: Experiences of African American Women

African American women faced unique challenges and opportunities during the Great Migration, as they navigated the complexities of urban life and sought to build better futures for themselves and their families.

1.1 Economic Survival

For many African American women, the Great Migration offered an opportunity to escape the economic hardships and limited opportunities of the rural South and seek better-paying jobs and greater economic independence in the North. Women found employment in a wide range of industries, including domestic work, manufacturing, and service, where they worked as maids, factory workers, nurses, and clerical staff, among other occupations. While employment provided women with a means of financial support and autonomy, it also subjected them to exploitation, discrimination, and harsh working conditions.

1.2 Family and Community

Despite the challenges they faced, African American women played a central role in maintaining family and community ties during the Great Migration, providing emotional support, caregiving, and leadership within their households and communities. Women were often the primary caregivers and breadwinners in their families, as they balanced work, household responsibilities, and community activism. Women's clubs, mutual aid societies, and church groups provided spaces for women to come together, share resources, and support one another in their struggles for survival and social change.

1.3 Cultural Expression

African American women also played a key role in preserving and promoting African American culture and identity during the Great Migration, as they celebrated their heritage through music, art, literature, and religious expression. Women's voices were heard in gospel choirs, literary salons, and community gatherings, where they shared stories, songs, and traditions passed down through generations. African American women artists, writers, and activists such as Zora Neale Hurston, Bessie Smith, and Ella Baker helped to shape the cultural and intellectual landscape of the Harlem Renaissance and beyond, using their creative talents and platforms to challenge stereotypes, inspire activism, and promote social change.

Section 2: Role of Women in Community Building

African American women played a central role in community building and social activism during the Great Migration, as they organized grassroots movements, built networks of support, and advocated for social justice and equality.

2.1 Community Organizing

Women's clubs, civic organizations, and social welfare agencies were instrumental in providing essential services and support to African American communities during the Great Migration, as they addressed the social, economic, and health needs of residents. Women organized community centers, settlement houses, and daycare centers to provide childcare, education, and recreation for children and families, while also advocating for improved housing, sanitation, and public services in African American neighborhoods.

2.2 Civil Rights Activism

African American women played a leading role in the Civil Rights Movement during the Great Migration, as they organized protests, boycotts, and voter registration drives to challenge racial segregation and discrimination in the North. Women such as Rosa Parks, Fannie Lou Hamer, and Ella Baker were key figures in the struggle for civil rights and social justice, using their voices and organizing skills to mobilize communities, build coalitions, and effect change. African American women's activism laid the groundwork for the broader Civil Rights Movement of the 1950s and 1960s, paving the way for landmark victories in desegregation, voting rights, and equal opportunity.

2.3 Labor Activism

African American women were also at the forefront of labor activism during the Great Migration, as they organized strikes, protests, and union campaigns to demand fair wages, decent working conditions, and respect on the job. Women such as A. Philip Randolph, Clara Lemlich, and Dorothy Bolden led efforts to organize domestic workers, factory workers, and service workers in the fight for economic justice and workers' rights. African American women's labor activism helped to raise awareness of the exploitation and discrimination faced by women workers in the North and paved the way for greater recognition and protections for workers' rights.

Section 3: Legacy and Impact

The contributions of African American women during the Great Migration have had a lasting impact on American society and culture, shaping the course of social change and advancing the cause of justice, equality, and opportunity for all.

3.1 Cultural Legacy

African American women's voices have been central to the preservation and promotion of African American culture and identity, as they have used their creative talents and platforms to celebrate their heritage, challenge stereotypes, and promote social change. Women writers, artists, musicians, and activists have played a vital role in shaping the cultural and intellectual landscape of the Harlem Renaissance, the Civil Rights Movement, and beyond, leaving a rich legacy of creativity, resilience, and resistance for future generations to draw upon.

3.2 Political Legacy

African American women's activism and leadership have had a profound impact on American politics and governance, as they have mobilized communities, built coalitions, and advocated for policies and programs that address the needs and concerns of marginalized communities. Women such as Shirley Chisholm, Barbara Jordan, and Fannie Lou Hamer broke barriers and shattered stereotypes as they fought for representation, inclusion, and social justice in the halls of power. African American women's political legacy continues to inspire new generations of activists and leaders to make their voices heard and demand change.

3.3 Social Legacy

African American women's contributions to community building and social activism have helped to create more equitable and inclusive communities, where all residents have access to the resources, opportunities, and support they need to thrive. Women's clubs, mutual aid societies, and grassroots organizations have provided essential services and support to African American communities during times of crisis and hardship, while also advocating for systemic change and social justice. African American women's social legacy continues to shape the work of community organizers, activists, and advocates who are committed to building a more just and equitable society for all.

In the chapters that follow, we will continue to explore the impact of the Great Migration and the contributions of African American women to American society and culture, examining the enduring legacy of their voices and their ongoing quest for justice, equality, and empowerment.

Chapter 12: Legacy and Impact

The Great Migration of African Americans from the rural South to the urban North was one of the most significant demographic shifts in American history, with far-reaching and enduring effects on African American communities, American society, and culture at large. In this chapter, we will explore the long-term legacy and impact of the Great Migration, examining its effects on African American communities, its influence on American culture, politics, and demographics, and its ongoing relevance in shaping the contemporary landscape of race and identity in America.

Section 1: Transforming African American Communities

The Great Migration transformed African American communities in profound and lasting ways, as millions of migrants sought new opportunities and forged new lives in the urban North.

1.1 Economic Mobility

One of the most significant effects of the Great Migration was the expansion of economic opportunities and upward mobility for African Americans in the North. Migrants found employment in a wide range of industries, including manufacturing, transportation, and service, where they gained access to higher wages, better working conditions, and opportunities for advancement. The migration spurred the growth of African American-owned businesses and institutions, as entrepreneurs and community leaders established businesses, churches, schools, and social organizations to serve the needs of the growing population.

1.2 Cultural Renaissance

The Great Migration also sparked a cultural renaissance in African American communities, as migrants brought with them their rich cultural heritage and traditions and infused Northern cities with new energy, creativity, and vitality. The Harlem Renaissance, a flowering of African American arts, literature, and culture centered in Harlem, New York, was one of the most notable manifestations of this cultural renaissance, as writers, artists, musicians, and intellectuals celebrated African American identity and explored themes of race, identity, and social justice in their work. The Harlem Renaissance had a profound influence on American culture and identity, helping to challenge stereotypes, promote cultural pride, and foster cross-cultural exchange and understanding.

1.3 Political Mobilization

The Great Migration also fueled the growth of African American political power and influence in the North, as migrants organized grassroots movements, voter registration drives, and advocacy campaigns to challenge racial discrimination and segregation and demand equal rights and opportunities. African American politicians, activists, and organizations such as the NAACP, the Urban League, and the Congress of Racial Equality (CORE) played a leading role in the struggle for civil rights and social justice, mobilizing communities, building coalitions, and effecting change at the local, state, and national levels. The migration helped to shift the balance of power in American politics and paved the way for landmark legislative victories such as the Civil Rights Act of 1964 and the Voting Rights Act of 1965.

Section 2: Influence on American Culture

The Great Migration had a profound influence on American culture, shaping the music, literature, art, and language of the 20th century and beyond.

2.1 Music and Dance

The Great Migration transformed the landscape of American music, as African American musicians and composers brought their unique musical traditions and styles to Northern cities, where they found new audiences and opportunities for artistic expression. Jazz, blues, gospel, and rhythm and blues emerged as dominant forms of African American music during the migration, as artists such as Louis Armstrong, Bessie Smith, Duke Ellington, and Mahalia Jackson helped to popularize these genres and elevate them to the status of global cultural icons. The migration also gave rise to new forms of dance and performance, such as the Lindy Hop and tap dancing, which became popular in clubs, theaters, and social gatherings across the country.

2.2 Literature and Art

The Great Migration inspired a wave of literary and artistic creativity among African American writers, artists, and intellectuals, who sought to capture the experiences and aspirations of migrants in their work. Writers such as Langston Hughes, Zora Neale Hurston, Richard Wright, and James Baldwin drew upon their own experiences and observations to create powerful and evocative works of fiction, poetry, and nonfiction that explored themes of race, identity, and social justice. African American artists such as Jacob Lawrence, Romare Bearden, and Augusta Savage used their talents to document the migration and its impact on African American communities, creating vibrant, expressive works of art that continue to resonate with audiences today.

2.3 Language and Vernacular

The Great Migration also had a profound impact on American language and vernacular, as African American migrants brought with them their distinctive speech patterns, dialects, and expressions, which enriched and diversified the linguistic landscape of Northern cities. African American vernacular English, or AAVE, became increasingly influential in American popular culture, as musicians, comedians, and writers incorporated its rhythms, cadences, and slang into their work, helping to shape the language of everyday speech and expression in America and beyond.

Section 3: Shifting Demographics and Identity

The Great Migration reshaped the demographic landscape of America, as millions of African Americans moved from the rural South to the urban North, where they sought new opportunities and freedom from the constraints of segregation and discrimination.

3.1 Urbanization

The Great Migration accelerated the process of urbanization in America, as African American migrants settled in Northern cities and formed vibrant, dynamic urban communities. Cities such as Chicago, New York, Detroit, and Philadelphia became centers of African American culture, commerce, and politics, as migrants built churches, schools, businesses, and social organizations to serve the needs of their communities. Urbanization brought with it new challenges and opportunities, as migrants grappled with issues such as housing segregation, overcrowding, poverty, and crime, while also forging new social networks, cultural identities, and collective identities.

3.2 Racial Identity

The Great Migration also had a profound impact on African American identity and consciousness, as migrants confronted the realities of racism, segregation, and discrimination in the North and sought to forge new identities and narratives of empowerment and resistance. African American migrants brought with them their own cultural traditions, customs, and values, which they adapted and reshaped to fit their new urban environments. The migration gave rise to new forms of cultural expression, solidarity, and collective action, as migrants organized grassroots movements, built community institutions, and asserted their rights and dignity in the face of systemic oppression and injustice.

3.3 National Identity

The Great Migration helped to redefine the meaning of American identity and citizenship, as African American migrants asserted their rightful place in the fabric of American society and demanded equal rights and opportunities under the law. The migration challenged prevailing notions of race, class, and citizenship in America, as African Americans asserted their agency and autonomy and challenged the racial hierarchies and systems of oppression that had long defined American life. The migration helped to foster a more inclusive and expansive vision of American identity, one that recognized the contributions and struggles of African Americans and affirmed their rightful place as full and equal members of the American community.

Section 4: Ongoing Relevance and Challenges

While the Great Migration transformed the lives of millions of African Americans and reshaped the cultural and political landscape of America, its legacy continues to reverberate in the present day, as communities grapple with ongoing challenges of racism, inequality, and injustice.

4.1 Economic Inequality

Despite the progress made since the Great Migration, African Americans continue to face significant disparities and challenges in the North, as they confront persistent barriers to economic opportunity, social mobility, and political representation. Structural racism, discriminatory policies, and systemic barriers continue to limit African American access to quality education, employment, healthcare, housing, and other essential resources and services, perpetuating cycles of poverty, segregation, and inequality in urban communities.

4.2 Racial Injustice

The legacy of racial injustice and discrimination that began with slavery and continued through the Jim Crow era and the Great Migration continues to shape the lived experiences of African Americans in the North and across the country. African Americans are disproportionately impacted by police violence, mass incarceration, environmental injustice, and other forms of systemic racism and oppression, as they continue to fight for justice, equality, and dignity in the face of ongoing threats to their lives, liberty, and pursuit of happiness.

4.3 Collective Resilience

Despite these challenges, African American communities remain resilient and resourceful, drawing upon the lessons and legacies of the Great Migration to navigate the complexities of contemporary life and work towards a more just and equitable future. Communities continue to organize, mobilize, and advocate for change, building coalitions, alliances, and movements to address the root causes of racial injustice and inequality and advance the cause of justice, equality, and opportunity for all.

In conclusion, the Great Migration of African Americans from the rural South to the urban North was a transformative and pivotal moment in American history, with profound and lasting effects on African American communities, American society, and culture. The migration reshaped the demographic, economic, and cultural landscape of America, as millions of migrants sought new opportunities and freedom from the constraints of segregation and discrimination. The migration helped to foster a more inclusive and expansive vision of American identity, one that recognized the contributions and struggles of African Americans and affirmed their rightful place as full and equal members of the American community. While the challenges of racism, inequality, and injustice persist, the legacy of the Great Migration continues to inspire new generations of activists, artists, and leaders to work towards a more just, equitable, and inclusive society for all.

Chapter 13: Remembering the Journey

The Great Migration was not only a historic event but also a deeply personal journey for the millions of African Americans who made the arduous decision to leave their homes in the rural South and seek new opportunities in the urban North. The memories and experiences of these migrants and their descendants provide invaluable insights into the motivations, challenges, and triumphs of the Great Migration, as well as its lasting impact on individuals, families, and communities. In this chapter, we will explore the oral histories and personal narratives of migrants and their descendants, examine the ways in which these stories are preserved and transmitted across generations, and consider the significance of remembering the journey for future generations.

Section 1: Oral Histories and Personal Narratives

The Great Migration was a transformative experience for millions of African Americans, as they left behind the familiar landscapes and social structures of the rural South and embarked on a journey into the unknown. Through oral histories, personal narratives, and family stories, we gain a deeper understanding of the motivations, challenges, and triumphs of the Great Migration, as well as its impact on individual lives and identities.

1.1 Motivations for Migration

The decision to migrate was driven by a complex interplay of economic, social, and political factors, as African Americans sought to escape poverty, oppression, and violence in the Jim Crow South and pursue new opportunities and freedoms in the North. Oral histories and personal narratives often highlight the push and pull factors that influenced migrants' decisions to leave, including the promise of better-paying jobs, improved living conditions, and greater educational and economic opportunities for themselves and their families.

1.2 Challenges and Triumphs

The journey North was fraught with challenges and obstacles, as migrants confronted discrimination, segregation, and violence at every turn. Oral histories and personal narratives document the struggles and sacrifices of migrants as they faced housing discrimination, employment barriers, and social isolation in their new urban environments. Yet, despite these challenges, migrants also found resilience, strength, and solidarity in their communities, as they built new lives and forged new identities in the face of adversity.

1.3 Legacy and Impact

The legacy of the Great Migration lives on in the stories and memories of migrants and their descendants, as they continue to draw upon their experiences and insights to navigate the complexities of contemporary life and work towards a more just and equitable future. Oral histories and personal narratives provide a powerful testament to the resilience, resourcefulness, and resilience of African American communities in the face of adversity, as well as the enduring legacy of the Great Migration in shaping the course of American history and identity.

Section 2: Preserving the Memory

The preservation of oral histories and personal narratives is essential for ensuring that the legacy of the Great Migration is not forgotten or erased, but rather celebrated and honored for future generations. Through a variety of mediums and platforms, individuals, organizations, and communities are working to collect, preserve, and share the stories of migrants and their descendants, ensuring that their voices and experiences are heard and remembered.

2.1 Archival Collections

Archival collections play a critical role in preserving the memory of the Great Migration, as they provide a repository for oral histories, personal narratives, photographs, documents, and other materials related to the migration experience. Libraries, museums, historical societies, and universities house extensive collections of primary sources that document the history and impact of the Great Migration, making them accessible to researchers, educators, and the general public for study, interpretation, and reflection.

2.2 Oral History Projects

Oral history projects are another important means of preserving the memory of the Great Migration, as they capture the stories and voices of migrants and their descendants through recorded interviews, testimonials, and conversations. Organizations such as the Smithsonian National Museum of African American History and Culture, the Library of Congress, and the Chicago History Museum have undertaken ambitious oral history projects to document the experiences of migrants and their descendants, creating rich and diverse archives of personal narratives that illuminate the human dimension of the migration experience.

2.3 Digital Archives and Exhibits

Digital archives and exhibits provide a dynamic and accessible platform for preserving and sharing the memory of the Great Migration with a global audience. Online repositories such as the Digital Public Library of America, the National Museum of African American History and Culture's "The Great Migration: A Story in Six Paintings," and the New York Public Library's "Schomburg Center for Research in Black Culture" offer virtual exhibitions, interactive timelines, and digitized collections of primary sources that bring the history and legacy of the Great Migration to life in new and innovative ways.

Section 3: Transmitting Across Generations

The transmission of oral histories and personal narratives across generations is essential for ensuring that the memory of the Great Migration endures and resonates with future generations. Families, communities, and educational institutions play a vital role in passing down stories, values, and traditions from one generation to the next, fostering a sense of connection, continuity, and resilience in the face of adversity.

3.1 Family Stories and Traditions

Family stories and traditions are the cornerstone of intergenerational transmission, as they provide a personal and intimate connection to the past and a sense of belonging and identity for future generations. Through family gatherings, reunions, and celebrations, families share stories, photos, and mementos of their ancestors and their migration experiences, keeping their memories alive and honoring their legacies for generations to come.

3.2 Community Celebrations and Events

Community celebrations and events are another important means of transmitting the memory of the Great Migration across generations, as they bring together individuals, families, and communities to commemorate and reflect upon the legacy of the migration experience. Annual festivals, parades, and commemorations such as the Chicago Defender's "Bud Billiken Parade and Picnic" and the Harlem Week celebrations in New York City provide opportunities for communities to come together, share stories, and celebrate the resilience and strength of African American culture and identity.

3.3 Educational Curricula and Programs

Educational curricula and programs play a critical role in transmitting the memory of the Great Migration to future generations, as they provide opportunities for students to learn about the history and impact of the migration experience in the classroom and beyond. Teachers, educators, and community leaders develop and implement curricula, lesson plans, and educational resources that incorporate primary sources, oral histories, and personal narratives into the curriculum, enabling students to engage critically with the history and legacy of the Great Migration and draw connections to their own lives and communities.

In conclusion, the memory of the Great Migration is a testament to the resilience, resourcefulness, and resilience of African American communities in the face of adversity. Through oral histories, personal narratives, and family stories, we gain a deeper understanding of the motivations, challenges, and triumphs of migrants and their descendants, as well as the enduring legacy of the migration experience in shaping the course of American history and identity. By preserving and transmitting these stories across generations, we honor the sacrifices and struggles of those who came before us and ensure that their voices and experiences are remembered and celebrated for generations to come.

Chapter 14: Continuing Struggles

Despite the promise of opportunity and freedom that drew millions of African Americans from the rural South to the urban North during the Great Migration, the journey towards equality and justice has been marked by persistent challenges and ongoing struggles. In this chapter, we will explore the enduring obstacles faced by African Americans in the North, as well as the continued efforts for social justice and equality in the face of systemic racism, economic inequality, and social injustice.

Section 1: Persistent Challenges

The legacy of slavery, segregation, and discrimination continues to shape the lived experiences of African Americans in the North, as they confront a range of persistent challenges and barriers to full participation in American society.

1.1 Economic Inequality

Economic inequality remains a pressing issue for African Americans in the North, as they continue to face disparities in income, employment, education, and wealth accumulation. African Americans are disproportionately represented in low-wage, precarious jobs with limited opportunities for advancement and are more likely to experience poverty, unemployment, and financial insecurity than their white counterparts. Structural barriers such as housing discrimination, educational inequity, and lack of access to capital and resources perpetuate economic inequality and restrict African American mobility and opportunity.

1.2 Housing Segregation

Housing segregation remains a pervasive and entrenched problem in Northern cities, as African Americans continue to face discrimination and exclusion in the housing market. Residential segregation concentrates poverty and disadvantage in African American neighborhoods, limiting access to quality housing, schools, healthcare, and other essential services. Discriminatory lending practices, redlining, and gentrification exacerbate housing insecurity and displacement, pushing African American families further to the margins of society and perpetuating cycles of poverty and inequality.

1.3 Educational Disparities

Educational disparities persist for African American students in the North, as they continue to face unequal access to quality schools, resources, and opportunities for academic achievement and success. African American students are disproportionately concentrated in underfunded, under-resourced schools with high rates of poverty, violence, and teacher turnover, which contribute to lower graduation rates, higher dropout rates, and limited pathways to higher education and career advancement. Structural inequities such as segregation, inadequate funding, and lack of access to culturally relevant curriculum and support services perpetuate educational disparities and hinder African American students' ability to reach their full potential.

1.4 Criminal Justice System

The criminal justice system remains a site of racial injustice and inequality for African Americans in the North, as they are disproportionately targeted, arrested, prosecuted, and incarcerated for minor offenses and nonviolent crimes. African Americans are more likely to be stopped, frisked, and detained by law enforcement, more likely to be charged with offenses, and more likely to receive harsher sentences and punishments than their white counterparts for similar offenses. Mass incarceration, racial profiling, and over-policing in African American communities perpetuate cycles of poverty, disenfranchisement, and social exclusion, contributing to the destabilization of families and communities and the erosion of trust and legitimacy in the criminal justice system.

Section 2: Ongoing Efforts for Social Justice and Equality

In the face of persistent challenges and barriers, African Americans in the North continue to organize, mobilize, and advocate for social justice and equality, drawing upon the lessons and legacies of the Great Migration to build coalitions, alliances, and movements for change.

2.1 Grassroots Organizing

Grassroots organizations play a critical role in advancing the struggle for social justice and equality in the North, as they mobilize communities, build power, and advocate for policy change at the local, state, and national levels. Organizations such as Black Lives Matter, the Movement for Black Lives, and local chapters of the NAACP, the Urban League, and other civil rights organizations lead campaigns for police reform, criminal justice reform, housing justice, education equity, and economic opportunity, mobilizing activists, allies, and supporters to demand accountability and systemic change.

2.2 Community Empowerment

Community empowerment is essential for addressing the root causes of inequality and injustice in African American communities in the North, as residents work together to build capacity, resilience, and self-determination. Community-based organizations, mutual aid networks, and grassroots initiatives provide essential services, resources, and support to African American communities, empowering residents to address their own needs and concerns and advocate for their own interests and priorities. Community empowerment strategies such as participatory budgeting, community land trusts, and restorative justice help to build social cohesion, trust, and solidarity, fostering a sense of belonging and ownership in African American neighborhoods and strengthening community resilience and resistance in the face of adversity.

2.3 Coalition Building

Coalition building is key to advancing the struggle for social justice and equality in the North, as African American activists and allies come together to build bridges, forge alliances, and mobilize collective action across lines of race, class, gender, and identity. Intersectional movements such as the Poor People's Campaign, the Fight for $15, and the reproductive justice movement bring together diverse constituencies to address the interconnected systems of oppression and exploitation that perpetuate inequality and injustice in American society. By building broad-based coalitions and alliances, activists and organizers are able to amplify their voices, leverage their power, and effect meaningful change in the pursuit of justice, equality, and liberation for all.

Section 3: Hope for the Future

Despite the formidable obstacles and challenges that remain, there is hope for the future as African Americans in the North continue to build upon the legacy of the Great Migration and work towards a more just, equitable, and inclusive society for all.

3.1 Youth Activism

Youth activism is a powerful force for social change in African American communities in the North, as young people mobilize, organize, and advocate for their own futures and the futures of their communities. Youth-led organizations such as the Youth Justice Coalition, the Dream Defenders, and the Sunrise Movement empower young people to take action on issues such as racial justice, climate justice, gun violence prevention, and immigrant rights, providing opportunities for leadership development, political engagement, and civic participation. By centering the voices and experiences of young people, youth activists are able to bring fresh perspectives, energy, and urgency to the struggle for social justice and equality, inspiring hope and optimism for the future.

3.2 Intergenerational Solidarity

Intergenerational solidarity is essential for building a movement for social justice and equality that spans generations and transcends divisions of age, race, and identity. Intergenerational organizations such as the Movement for Black Lives, the National Association for the Advancement of Colored People (NAACP), and the American Civil Liberties Union (ACLU) bring together activists, organizers, and advocates of all ages to work towards common goals and objectives, fostering mutual respect, understanding, and support across generations. By sharing knowledge, skills, and resources, intergenerational activists are able to build upon the successes and lessons of the past, while also envisioning and creating a brighter future for generations to come.

3.3 Collective Resilience

Collective resilience is the bedrock of the African American struggle for social justice and equality in the North, as communities draw upon their shared history, culture, and values to withstand and overcome adversity. In the face of persistent challenges and barriers, African Americans in the North continue to demonstrate resilience, resourcefulness, and resolve, as they build networks of support, solidarity, and resistance to confront systemic racism, economic inequality, and social injustice. By standing together, speaking out, and taking action, African Americans in the North are able to create spaces of belonging, agency, and empowerment, where all residents have the opportunity to thrive and fulfill their potential.

In conclusion, the struggle for social justice and equality continues for African Americans in the North, as they confront persistent challenges and obstacles in their quest for freedom, dignity, and opportunity. By organizing, mobilizing, and advocating for change, African Americans in the North are able to build upon the legacy of the Great Migration and work towards a more just, equitable, and inclusive society for all. Through grassroots organizing, community empowerment, and coalition building, African Americans in the North are able to amplify their voices, leverage their power, and effect meaningful change in the pursuit of justice, equality, and liberation for all.

Chapter 15: Reflections and Conclusion

As we come to the conclusion of our exploration of the Great Migration and its impact on African American communities in the North, it is essential to reflect on the lessons learned from this historic journey and consider its relevance for contemporary society. In this final chapter, we will examine the enduring legacy of the Great Migration, draw insights from its lessons, and contemplate the aspirations and challenges facing African American communities in the 21st century.

Section 1: Lessons Learned

The Great Migration stands as a testament to the resilience, courage, and determination of African American communities in the face of adversity. Through their experiences, migrants and their descendants have imparted valuable lessons that continue to resonate with us today.

1.1 Resilience in the Face of Adversity

One of the most enduring lessons of the Great Migration is the resilience of African American communities in the face of systemic racism, economic hardship, and social injustice. Despite the many challenges and obstacles they faced, migrants and their descendants demonstrated remarkable resilience, resourcefulness, and resolve as they navigated the complexities of urban life and forged new paths for themselves and future generations. Their stories remind us of the power of perseverance, determination, and community solidarity in overcoming adversity and achieving collective liberation.

1.2 Collective Action and Solidarity

The Great Migration also highlights the importance of collective action and solidarity in effecting social change and advancing the cause of justice and equality. Migrants and their descendants organized grassroots movements, built community institutions, and forged alliances with allies and partners to challenge racial discrimination, segregation, and oppression in the North. Their efforts remind us of the power of unity, mobilization, and coalition building in confronting systemic injustice and building a more just and equitable society for all.

1.3 Celebration of Culture and Identity

Another important lesson of the Great Migration is the celebration of culture and identity as sources of strength, resilience, and resistance. Migrants and their descendants brought with them their rich cultural heritage and traditions, which they preserved, adapted, and transformed in their new urban environments. Through music, art, literature, dance, and other forms of cultural expression, they affirmed their identities, challenged stereotypes, and asserted their humanity in the face of dehumanizing racism and oppression. Their creative expressions remind us of the power of culture, art, and storytelling in fostering resilience, resistance, and collective healing.

Section 2: Relevance Today

While the Great Migration occurred over a century ago, its legacy continues to reverberate in contemporary society, shaping the aspirations and challenges of African American communities in the 21st century.

2.1 Economic Inequality and Opportunity

Economic inequality remains a pressing issue for African American communities in the North, as they continue to face disparities in income, wealth, employment, and access to quality education and healthcare. Structural barriers such as housing discrimination, educational inequity, and lack of access to capital and resources perpetuate economic inequality and restrict African American mobility and opportunity. Addressing these disparities requires comprehensive solutions that address the root causes of poverty, discrimination, and social exclusion and create pathways to economic empowerment, wealth creation, and social mobility for all.

2.2 Racial Injustice and Equity

Racial injustice and inequality persist in American society, as African Americans continue to face discrimination, marginalization, and violence in their interactions with law enforcement, the criminal justice system, and other institutions of power and authority. Structural racism, implicit bias, and systemic barriers perpetuate disparities in policing, sentencing, and incarceration, contributing to the criminalization and dehumanization of African American communities. Achieving racial equity and justice requires transformative change that dismantles systems of oppression, invests in community-based solutions, and centers the voices and experiences of those most impacted by racism and injustice.

2.3 Political Empowerment and Representation

Political empowerment and representation are essential for advancing the interests and priorities of African American communities in the North, as they continue to advocate for policies and programs that address their needs and concerns. Voter suppression, gerrymandering, and other forms of voter disenfranchisement undermine African American political power and participation, limiting their ability to influence decision-making and shape public policy. Building a more inclusive and representative democracy requires efforts to expand access to the ballot, increase voter turnout and engagement, and promote diverse and equitable representation in all levels of government.

Section 3: Looking Towards the Future

As we look towards the future, it is essential to remain hopeful and optimistic about the possibilities for positive change and transformation in African American communities in the North.

3.1 Youth Leadership and Activism

Youth leadership and activism are critical for driving social change and building a more just and equitable future for all. Young people are leading the charge for racial justice, environmental justice, gender equity, and other pressing issues, using their voices, energy, and creativity to mobilize communities, challenge the status quo, and envision alternative futures. By empowering and supporting young leaders, we can cultivate a new generation of change-makers and advocates who will continue the struggle for justice, equality, and liberation.

3.2 Intergenerational Solidarity and Collaboration

Intergenerational solidarity and collaboration are essential for building bridges, fostering understanding, and amplifying the voices and experiences of African American communities across generations. By sharing knowledge, skills, and resources, older and younger generations can learn from one another, support one another, and work together to address the root causes of inequality and injustice in society. By building strong and resilient intergenerational networks, we can create spaces of belonging, agency, and empowerment where all members of the community can thrive and fulfill their potential.

3.3 Collective Action and Community Building

Collective action and community building are key to effecting meaningful and sustainable change in African American communities in the North. By coming together, organizing, and mobilizing around shared goals and priorities, communities can leverage their collective power and resources to address systemic injustices, build resilience, and create opportunities for social, economic, and political empowerment. By building strong and inclusive communities, we can create spaces of belonging, solidarity, and resistance where all members feel valued, supported, and empowered to shape their own destinies and the future of their communities.

In conclusion, the Great Migration and its legacy continue to shape the aspirations and challenges of African American communities in the North in the 21st century. By drawing upon the lessons learned from the past, we can confront the persistent obstacles and injustices facing our communities and work towards a future of justice, equality, and liberation for all. Through collective action, community building, and intergenerational solidarity, we can create a more just, equitable, and inclusive society where all members have the opportunity to thrive and fulfill their potential. As we reflect on the journey of the Great Migration and look towards the future, let us remain committed to the principles of resilience, solidarity, and justice that have guided us on this historic journey and continue to inspire us in the pursuit of a brighter tomorrow.

Don't miss out!

Visit the website below and you can sign up to receive emails whenever Michael Johnson publishes a new book. There's no charge and no obligation.

https://books2read.com/r/B-A-OREFB-CJYAD

BOOKS 2 READ

Connecting independent readers to independent writers.

Did you love *The Great Migration*? Then you should read *The Gold Rush*[1] by Michael Johnson!

[2]

"Delve into the frenzy of America's pursuit of wealth in the West with 'The Gold Rush.' From the spark of opportunity at Sutter's Mill to the decline of mining, explore the journey westward, the birth of boomtowns, and the environmental and social impact of this transformative era. Discover the enduring cultural legacy and lessons learned from this captivating chapter in American history."

---

1. https://books2read.com/u/47JEZR

2. https://books2read.com/u/47JEZR

About the Author

Michael Johnson is a distinguished historian specializing in American history. With a degree in History from Harvard University, Johnson's work delves into pivotal moments, figures, and themes shaping the United States. He has authored numerous acclaimed books, offering insightful perspectives and engaging narratives. Johnson's commitment to meticulous scholarship and compelling storytelling has earned him widespread acclaim in the field. Passionate about sharing his expertise, he frequently engages in lectures and public events to foster a deeper appreciation for America's past.